Agility

A step-by-step guide

Patrick Holden and John Gilbert

RINGPRESS

DEDICATION

We dedicate this book with affection to
Peter Meanwell, the founder of Agility.

ACKNOWLEDGEMENTS

We are grateful for the help received from:

The Kennel Club, including their permission to include
copyright data from their *Kennel Club Year Book*.

Tony Griffin, and Daventry Dog Training Club.

Vanessa Hoare, for making sense of our jottings.

*The 'he' pronoun is used throughout this book in favour of the rather
impersonal 'it', but no gender bias is intended.*

COVER PHOTOGRAPHY

Peg (Foxtwist Friday Feeling), owned, bred,
and handled by Jackie Bromwich.

Design: Sara Howell

**Published by Ringpress Books,
Vincent Lane, Dorking, Surrey,
RH4 3YX, England**

First published 2001
© Interpet Publishing. All rights reserved

ISBN 1 86054 044 9

Printed and bound in Hong Kong through Printworks International Ltd.

About the Authors

Patrick Holden is one of the country's leading dog trainers, with more than 25 years of experience. Patrick's enviable career in Obedience and Working Trials provided him with a head start in Agility. He trained his Golden Retriever, Ob. Ch. Melnola Bramble CDEx-TDEx, to become the first, and, so far, the only, Golden of all time to qualify at top-level Obedience and Working Trials.

It was with Bramble that Patrick entered the world of Agility, enlisting the help of John Gilbert. Bramble achieved considerable success by reaching the finals of the UK Super-Dog event, completing the Agility course within the time limit and without faults.

John Gilbert began his career as a dog trainer in 1967, but it was in 1978 that John's career really took off. With Becky, his German Shepherd, John was one of the first top competitors, qualifying for the Olympia finals six times as well as winning many other competitions.

John was instrumental in forming the rules of the sport and became one of the first people to judge it. He has since judged in more than 19 countries in the world.

In the late 1980s, John established his own training centre for Obedience and Agility, and now travels the world, teaching Agility judges, instructors and handlers. He is the chief Editor of *Agility Voice* magazine.

Contents

Foreword

I thoroughly recommend *Agility: A Step-by-Step Guide* to you. While it is primarily intended for beginners to the sport, others, particularly at club level, may find it useful to improve their performance. It will aid your Agility aspirations, whatever your goals.

It was in the autumn of 1977 that John Varley of the Crufts Show Committee asked me to devise an event to fill 20 minutes in the main ring, while Best in Show awards were being prepared. My brief was to hold the spectators' interest, and something along the lines of horse-jumping was suggested.

To help put it all together, I recruited my closest Working Trial friends (Lincoln club: Albert Davies, Stuart Gillam, Kevin Foster, Gerald Fox; Yorkshire Working Trials Society: Fred Welham, Trevor Jones, Don Horsfall, Jane Aldred, Brenda Lambert, Liz Hancock).

Having designed the equipment, I asked the Lincoln club to build two sets so that both clubs could practise. This we did, and at Crufts Dog Show 1978, Agility as a competition was seen for the first time.

WORLDWIDE RECOGNITION

During 1979, the UK Kennel Club was to make official rules for the sport, and it was at this stage that Peter Lewis became involved

in the rule-making body. Becoming very enthusiastic, he was quickly a successful competitor and innovator of many of the customs and practices that were needed to accompany the basic rules. This led him to introduce other countries of the world to this fledgling sport. Subsequently, he became very friendly with John Gilbert as they shared a like mind about Agility's future.

In 1983, after also recruiting Dave Ray into their plan, together with others, they set up an Agility club on a national basis. This club was an instant success and from it, through various courses and seminars, many of their ideas were put into practice.

Agility is a fun sport that can be enjoyed by dogs of all shapes and sizes.

MOVING FORWARD

With the exception of Don Horsfall, those of us who started the sport were not involved after the first two years, and therefore, Peter Lewis and John Gilbert were to take the sport forward. Peter was by now regularly visiting other countries and soon John was joining him.

Now the world plays this sport, and, indeed, it has its own World Championships. I have been very pleased to watch its growth, which, looking back to the early days, is something we did not expect. Not everyone aspires to such dizzy heights as playing on the world stage, and such is Agility's nature that fun can be had at any level. In this book, the authors clearly state that there is room for all, no matter whether they just want to have fun with their dog or to take on the best.

It is the fun aspect that is important – for dogs and owners alike. It is what I believed in the beginning and still do today. So, if this book also helps you to start or improve your dog's Agility career, then the authors have achieved their objective.

Peter Meanwell
(The founder of Agility)

1 Introducing Agility

Agility was born in 1978, when a demonstration of the sport was staged at Crufts, in the UK. A further demonstration was included in the Olympia International Horse Show the following year. The sport was so well received, on both occasions, that it quickly developed into a fully-fledged competitive sport, established and run by the Kennel Club. Agility has now been awarded Championship status in Britain, bringing it into line with the other dog sports of Obedience, Working Trials, Field Trials and Breed Shows. Today, Agility has become a popular sport all over the world.

WHAT IS AGILITY?

Agility is a canine sport in which the dog has to negotiate a variety of obstacles laid out in a

Agility is an international sport with a worldwide following.

The enthusiasm of the canine competitors is always apparent, as shown by this Cavalier King Charles Spaniel.

course. The handler runs much of the course with the dog, guiding him in the right direction and over each obstacle. The course has to be completed either within a set time, or in as fast a time as possible. The winning team is normally the one with the best time and the fewest penalties.

Each course consists of up to 20 different obstacles. The qualities of each obstacle (e.g. height) are adjustable according to the size of the dog. For example, the height of a jump will be reduced for smaller dogs. Each team begins the course

with a clean sheet, incurring a penalty – of five marks – every time the dog makes a mistake, such as refusing to negotiate an obstacle. The team which incurs fewest penalties, and completes the course in the fastest time, is the winner.

THE RULING BODY

Agility competitions are usually affiliated to the kennel club of each country, with each club having its own set of rules. However, the differences are minor – such as different heights for jumping obstacles – and the obstacles themselves are much the same the world over, making Agility suitable for the World Championships. If you are interested in taking up Agility, and wish to know more about the specific rules and regulations applicable to you, contact your national kennel club.

In the UK, since the Kennel Club incorporated Agility in its list of approved sports, more than 230 Agility clubs, all over the country, have registered. There are also numerous private clubs and instructors. One of the reasons behind the sport's popularity is that it is suitable for dogs and handlers of any ability. An example of the philosophy behind Agility can be seen in an extract from the UK's *Kennel Club Year Book:*

"Agility Tests are considered to be 'fun competitions', designed for enjoyment by competitors, their dogs, and for appeal to spectators... Nothing may be included in an Agility Test which could endanger the safety of the dogs competing, the handlers or the spectators."

Once fully grown, all types of dog can compete in Agility.

TAKING PART

Many of those attracted to Agility never take up the sport. This is because of a common misconception that Agility is suitable only for highly trained, large, athletic dogs. This is far from the truth.

Whether pure-bred or mongrel, large or small, your dog is likely to be a suitable candidate for Agility. The most important specifications are those of age and fitness.

Most national kennel clubs will not allow dogs to compete unless they are over a certain age. For example, the UK Kennel Club excludes any dog under 18 months, while the American Kennel Club has a lower limit of 12 months old. This is because most dogs will not reach maturity until 12-18 months of age.

Even when he appears to have reached full size, it is important to remember that your dog's joints and ligaments are still forming. Overexercising your pet at this stage can cause permanent damage.

SIZE MATTERS

For the purposes of training and

Obstacles are lowered for the mini breeds such as this West Highland White Terrier.

competition, there are three classes of size. In the UK, these are:

- **Standard:** over 17 in (43.18 cm), at the withers.
- **Midi:** between 15 in (38.1 cm) and 17 in (43.18 cm).
- **Mini:** under 15 in (38.1 cm).

Obstacles are adjusted according to each class, and your dog will compete against other dogs in his category. Make sure you measure your dog very carefully. Check with your national kennel club for the size categories specific to your country.

The vast majority of dogs fall into the standard category. Small dogs (e.g. Papillons) have their own, lower obstacles. Large dogs (e.g. Rottweilers) can do well, but very large dogs (e.g. St. Bernards) may have difficulties. Bulky dogs may not have the same degree of flexibility as their smaller counterparts.

BREED CHOICE

The UK Kennel Club allows both pure-bred dogs and cross-breeds to enter Agility. Other countries may permit pure-bred animals only. Some breeds are reputedly more difficult to train than others, but this is largely down to the dog's individual character and training.

FITNESS AND TRAINING

Unruly dogs are *not* suitable candidates for Agility. However, as long as a good standard of basic control has been achieved, no special abilities are required to take up the sport. The instructor of your chosen club will train you and your dog to the necessary standard. He may also advise you about diet and exercise regimes.

It is worth following these programmes even if you choose to participate at a fun level only. A good diet and an active

The larger bulkier breeds, like this Rottweiler, can be successful, but they do not have the speed or the flexibility of some of the smaller breeds.

Some breeds can be more of a challenge to train, but this Staffordshire Bull Terrier proves that the dog's character is the most important consideration.

lifestyle will help your dog to live to a ripe old age, as well as improving his quality of life.

THE HANDLER

With enthusiasm and instruction, most dog owners are able to participate in Agility.

The age of Agility handlers ranges from 6 to 70 plus. As with all sports, there are advantages to starting at a young age. Seniority is no bar, however, and Agility boasts top-level competitors in their 50s and 60s. We also have a competitor who is 56 years of age and the proud owner of two artificial hips!

You do not need to be a super-fit athlete to participate in Agility, but a basic level of fitness is necessary. Remember that you will have to run the course with your dog.

DEDICATION

To get the maximum enjoyment from Agility it helps to be competitive and dedicated. By striving to improve, you will achieve better results and higher rewards. However, the emphasis should be on fun, not trophies. It also helps to have the right dog. All these factors determine at which level you choose to compete, whether that be at the

A SPORT FOR ALL

Old and young alike can compete in the sport, as long as they have
a basic level of fitness.

village fête or at Crufts – the
Agility equivalent of Wimbledon
– or at a World Championship.

FINDING OUT MORE

If you want to try Agility, we
strongly recommend that you
enrol with a registered club
and an approved instructor. By
doing so you will be assured of
having the correct, well-main-
tained equipment, and expert
supervision. It cannot be stressed
enough that this book is no sub-
stitute for a qualified instructor

and regular supervised practice.
Agility, like any active sport, has
its share of injuries, and tackling
obstacles incorrectly may result
in nasty accidents. Safety must
come first at all times, and a
good club will always take this
into account.

There is almost certainly an
Agility club close to your home,
and club members will be
delighted to welcome you to a
session or to have a trial run.
Contact your national kennel
club for details of clubs in

A training club will give both you and your dog the help and guidance you need.

your area.

If you are not sure that you want to join a club at this moment, there is no shortage of Agility competitions which you can attend. Every year there are several big events in the canine calendar, such as Crufts, Discover Dogs, and the Olympia International Horse Show in the UK, or Westminster in the US. These all hold Agility demonstrations. Demos are also held at various Championship shows throughout the year.

Every year, the World Championships take place. For those unable to travel to the hosting venue, these displays are often broadcast on television.

2 Preparing For Agility

Although there is no need to have trained your dog to the highest level, you should not enrol at Agility classes unless you and your dog have learned basic training and control. Your local club will expect this. Remember that an ill-behaved dog is disruptive and unpleasant for all concerned.

TRAINING METHODS

Modern instructors rely on positive, reward-based techniques, and we recommend these. There are three acceptable methods in use today, which are normally used in conjunction with each other. There is also one negative training method.

- **Positive shaping/reinforcement:** Achieving the desired action through training, and then reinforcing with rewards.
- **Diversion:** Preventing unwanted behaviour by training an alternative response.

- **Containment:** Using neutral means to avoid unwanted actions.
- **Aversion:** Using negative means to change unwanted actions.

REWARD-BASED TRAINING

Positive-shaping methods have two elements. The first is to shape (teach) the dog how to perform the action correctly. The second is to reinforce that shaping, conditioning your dog by giving him a reward each time he behaves correctly. With your instructor, find a reward that your dog finds irresistible. Rewards can take the form of play (vigorous, chase or tug, or retrieve with a favourite toy), food treats, praise, or clicks from a clicker-training device.

In Agility, it is helpful to train with a toy, such as a ball on a rope. This encourages an association in the dog's mind

REWARD-BASED TRAINING

A ball on a rope makes an ideal training toy.

A game with the training toy is the dog's reward for a correct response.

between training and positive play, with the toy/reward acting as a lure when thrown through tunnels and hoops, etc. If you decide to use food rewards – always good for motivation – use something like cheese or baked

Diversion distracts the dog from undesirable behaviour. For example, a dog cannot bark if he is holding a dumb-bell!

liver, i.e. something that is tasty and easy to swallow for your dog, and small and easy to carry in your pocket for you. When the desired action has been learned and reinforced, your rewards can be given less frequently and at random. Never stop them altogether.

DIVERSION

Diversion works by dissuading a dog from an unwanted action by replacing it with a desired behaviour. For example, if you want to stop your dog barking, ask him to "Hold" an article in his mouth. Most dogs are unable to continue barking if they have their mouths full!

CONTAINMENT

Containment prevents unwanted behaviour before it arises. For example, walking on a lead prevents your dog from running off, while a Halti™ collar inhibits pulling. As a would-be Agility participant, the most important containment device is your crate. In the car it provides a safe means of transporting your dog from venue to venue. Once at the venue, the crate can be left in the car, or taken out and used to

The seasoned Agility competitor is quite content to be confined to his crate when travelling, or for short periods when you are at the show.

keep your dog safely confined while you wait your turn during training sessions or competition.

AVERSION

Aversion should only be used when all else has failed. It works by forming an association in the dog's mind between an undesirable action and its unpleasant consequences. For example, chewing can be stopped by impregnating the chewed object with an unpleasant taste or smell. Likewise, spraying a jet of water at your dog's face (from a squeezy bottle, for example), may discourage him from chasing or barking at another animal.

BASIC TRAINING

Training your dog in and around your home is essential, and we strongly recommend that you join a club for basic training and socialisation. Among the basic training skills, which your club and instructor will expect from your dog, are:

- Toilet training.
- Socialisation, with other people and with other dogs.
- Collar-and-lead familiarisation. This is needed for basic control, particularly during the excitement of an Agility session.
- Name recognition. Your dog must know his name and

19

A well-trained dog is a must if you want to be successful in Agility.

respond to it *instantly*, by looking at you when you call it, and waiting for your next command.

If you can, enrol on your kennel club's Good Citizen Scheme. This applies to everyone, no matter how old your dog or what breed (or cross-breed) he may be. Contact your national kennel club for more information.

BASIC CONTROL

In addition to basic training skills, before joining a club that offers Agility only, you should train your dog in these exercises:

- **Recall**, when your dog comes back to you when you call, is a must (page 22).
- **Staying put**. Wait is essential, Settle and Stay are useful.
- **Positions**. Down is essential, Sit, and Stand are helpful.
- **Heelwork**. This is when your dog moves with you, on both sides, first at a walking pace and then at running (page 21).
- **Sendaway**. This is an essential exercise where your dog moves ahead of you, on both sides. Learning to redirect your dog when he is ahead of you, to the left and to the right, is also helpful (page 23).

Your training club will also help you and your dog to learn the necessary exercises, using the positive methods described above.

Now you are ready to begin Agility.

HEELWORK

The dog must learn to stay in position, working on
both sides of the handler, and at different paces.

*Above left: The dog's attention
is focused on the handler while
he comes into position.*

*Above right: The position is
maintained with a change of
direction.*

*Left: The dog responds to
the change of pace, still
maintaining his heelwork
position.*

THE RECALL

A strong, positive reaction to the Recall is essential.

1. The dog stays in position when commanded to Wait.

2. The combination of the verbal command and the body language encourages the dog to come.

3. The dog comes in fast and straight.

4. The exercise is completed with a Sit in the Present position.

SENDAWAY

An excellent way of training Sendaway is to direct your dog towards his food bowl.

3 Getting Started

A small number of preparations will help you to get off to a flying start in Agility. Firstly, you need to choose a good club and to acquire the right equipment. Secondly, you need to choose the commands and signals which you are going to use in Agility, applying them to your basic control commands.

CHOOSING AN INSTRUCTOR

Having made a shortlist of clubs in your area, you need to visit each one in turn. It is very important that you see the instructor at work. Training methods are variable, and it is for the instructor and handler to decide what works for each individual dog. However, there are no excuses for using cruel training methods, and if you see an instructor using a 'yank and shout' approach, or any means of physical abuse, decline membership of that club.

In the UK there are special classes for young people, and anyone under the age of 12 should choose an instructor who is registered with the Kennel Club Junior Organisation. Contact the KC to obtain details of KCJO instructors in your area. Many registered instructors train adult contenders also, which makes Agility an ideal family activity.

EQUIPMENT

Choosing the right equipment will not only help the training run more smoothly, it will also reduce the risk of accidents, and give you greater control over your dog.

- Your dog's equipment should include a collar, a training lead, a water bowl, and a towel.
- Your 'kit' should contain appropriate clothing which is comfortable and casual.

Jogging pants or tracksuits are ideal. Anything which constricts your breathing or movement is unsuitable, as are skirts – they tend to flap in your dog's face.

- Footwear must be trainers or waterproof shoes with a good grip. High-heeled shoes, flip-flops or sandals are completely unsuitable, as are Wellington boots, which do not give a sufficient grip. One of our clubs, whose training field is often waterlogged, insists on all members wearing football boots with studs for grip.

Suitable clothing that does not restrict movement is essential for the handler.

- A dog crate or cage.
- A plentiful supply of rewards. A toy that can be thrown or used as a tug-toy is useful in Agility, and we recommend this. A clicker can also be very successful. However, clickers depend on very accurate timing and need to be the subject of discrete training.
- Various obstacles. As time passes, and you become more experienced, you may like to practise some obstacles at home. Your club may let you borrow equipment, or, should you wish to purchase your own, your club will give you the name of a reliable supplier.

BODY LANGUAGE

Dogs communicate using body language. Every snarl, growl and wag of the tail carries a message. You should never forget that your posture and mannerisms will convey as much meaning to your dog as the vocal commands you use.

If you are able to control your body language, it can prove an invaluable training aid. 'Encouraging' body language (bouncy, urgent, enthusiastic) and 'approving' body language

As you become more experienced, you will want to have equipment to practise on at home.

(smiles, welcoming posture, etc.) will help to shape your dog's behaviour as much as his other rewards. Likewise, 'disapproval' (frowning, or drooping posture) will alert your dog that he has done wrong.

SIGNALS AND COMMANDS

Although you are free to choose your own commands, you will find that most people use the same ones. This avoids confusion. Your club's instructor will inform you of the protocols used in your particular club, but, as a general guide, common commands are listed below.

Signals also play an important role in Agility training. They should be used in conjunction with voice commands as each reinforces the other.

GENERAL TIPS

- Whichever command you choose, be consistent. It does not matter whether your voice commands are in English or Swahili as long as your dog has been trained to respond to them. Always use the same commands and the same tone of voice.
- Create a list of your command words. Circulate copies to the rest of your family and to your instructor – basically, anyone involved in training your dog.

SIGNALS AND COMMANDS

Action: Recall

Signal Command: Arms apart, then brought to a 'V' shape over the groin, with the palms of the hands facing inwards

Voice Command: "Come"

Action: Wait

Signal Command: Arm bent from elbow, palm up

Voice Command: "Wait"

Action: Go down or drop

Signal Command: Arm pushes down, with the palm faced downwards

Voice Command: "Down"

Action: Go on/Away

Signal Command: Underarm push, pointing hand and arm in the required direction

Voice Command: "Go" or "Away"

Action: Go left

Signal Command:
Left arm extended in
the required direction

Voice Command:
"Back" or "Left"

Action: Go right

Signal Command:
Right arm extended
in the required
direction

Voice Command:
"This way" or
"Right"

Action: Jump over

Signal Command:
Point above the jump
with relevant arm
(i.e. the arm nearest
the obstacle)

Voice Command:
"Over"

Action: Walk/Contacts

Signal Command: Point
to contact points. Use
"Walk", "Down" or
"Steady" to slow the dog
down and to ensure that
he touches all the contact
points.

Voice Command:
"Walk", "Down" and
"Steady"

Action: Weave through poles

Signal Command: Point to the first pole and then to each gap, moving your hand over the poles

Voice Command: "Weave"

Action: Run through tunnels

Signal Command: Point at the tunnel entrance, followed by underarm push to indicate going through the tunnel

Voice Command: "Tunnel"/"Through"

Action: Jump through tyre/hoop
Signal Command: Point to the hole in the tyre/hoop
Voice Command: "Hoop"/"Through"

Action: Release command
Signal Command: Give the dog his reward
Voice Command: "Off"/"Get it"

4 Hurdle Jumps

Teaching your dog to jump hurdles is the first stage of Agility training. It will help to improve your dog's fitness, and is required for many of the other obstacles.

BASIC HURDLES

The basic hurdle consists of two uprights supporting a crossbar or pole, which, if knocked, is easily displaced by the dog.

The maximum height of a hurdle is 2 ft 6 in (76.2 cm) for standard dogs, 1 ft 8 in (50.8 cm) for midi dogs, and 1 ft 3 in (38.1 cm) for mini dogs.

It is easier to begin training using a hurdle without wings (i.e. without any supports attached to the uprights), since the absence of wings gives the handler much more room to move.

PHASE ONE

- Set the crossbar at its lowest height.
- With your dog on his training lead, command "Sit", so that he is facing the hurdle.
- Command your dog to Wait, using the voice command and the hand signal (see page 27).
- Walking backwards, move round to the other side of the hurdle. Keep a loose hold of the training lead, but ensure that it runs freely over the hurdle bar.
- Using the basic control Recall method, command your dog to Come. At the same time, tug on the lead, take a step backwards, and bring your hands to your groin in the V-shaped hand signal for Recall.
- Reward your dog.
- Repeat the exercise until your dog is confident.
- Raise the height of the crossbar, in gradual stages, until your dog is jumping it at maximum height.

TEACHING HURDLES

The instructor stays on one side of the hurdle with the dog, who is on the lead. The handler commands "Wait".

Using the basic Recall, the dog is commanded to Come.

PHASE TWO

- Set the crossbar to its lowest height.
- Ask your dog to Sit facing the hurdle. This time, allow enough room for a short walk-up.
- With your dog on your left side, walk with him towards the hurdle.
- When you reach the hurdle encourage him to jump (at this stage he should automatically attempt the jump). As he jumps, say "Over", and reward him by instantly throwing his toy ahead of him.
- Reward his success.
- Repeat the exercise, this time with your dog on your right-hand side.
- When your dog appears equally confident on either side of you, gradually raise the height of the crossbar to the maximum height for his size.
- Increase your dog's speed over the hurdle, until you are both running.

PHASE THREE

- Set up two hurdles, approximately 4 m apart. Set the

The dog, now off-lead, is commanded to Wait.

The command "Over" is used as the dog jumps.

A food reward can be used to encourage the dog to hurdle.

The command "Over" is used as the dog jumps and he is instantly rewarded.

Some dogs need an incentive to tackle obstacles. In this case, a ball, or a training toy, can be used as a lure.

crossbars at their lowest height.

- Tell your dog to Sit, facing hurdle one.
- Walk around between the two hurdles and call him over the first hurdle.
- Step aside, to allow him past you, then say "Over", give your hand signal, and send your dog over the second hurdle, as in phase two.
- Reward and repeat, this time with your dog on your other side.
- Gradually increase the height of the crossbar and the speed with which your dog tackles these hurdles.

PROBLEMS AND TIPS

- If your dog refuses to jump, the hurdle may be too high. Lower the crossbar to the ground, if necessary, and be more encouraging.
- If your dog will not wait before jumping, ask your instructor or a friend to restrain him. Eventually, he will understand that he must wait.
- If your dog knocks down the pole, lower it slightly before he tries again. The correct

type of pole will not hurt him, but he may find it off-putting. Lowering the crossbar will prevent your dog from developing any anxiety about the hurdles.

- Revert to phase one and/or lower the crossbar, if you lose control at any time.

WALLS AND BRUSH FENCES

These obstacles are variants of the basic hurdle, but, instead of comprising two uprights and a crossbar, walls and brush fences have a solid base. *The Kennel Club Year Book* states that the solid body of these obstacles must be topped with displace-able units. This is so that the dog does not injure himself if he misjudges the obstacle and knocks his legs.

Neither the wall nor the brush fence should be tackled until your dog has fully mastered the basic hurdle, i.e. when he can clear the hurdle at full height, on the run, on either side of you, following only your voice command and hand signal.

PHASE ONE

- Lower the wall as far as possible.

The brush fence is just one of several variants of the basic hurdle.

- With your dog on his lead, tell him to Sit facing the wall.
- Command him to Wait, and walk backwards around the wall so that you are facing your dog. Make sure that the lead is trailing over the obstacle.
- Recall your dog over the hurdle.
- Reward him when he does so.
- Once he is confident, add the displaceable bricks to the wall, so that the jump becomes gradually higher.

PHASE TWO
- Lower the height of the wall.

- Sit your dog facing the wall, and stand by his side.
- Walk with your dog towards the wall, and encourage him to jump once he reaches the obstacle.
- Say "Over" as your dog jumps. Use his toy as a lure.
- Reward your dog by lobbing his toy over the hurdle and in front of him.
- Repeat the exercise, this time with your dog on your other side.
- Once your pet is confident on either side, replace the bricks on the wall and repeat the exercise and reward.

- Gradually increase the speed at which your dog tackles the obstacle.

PROBLEMS AND TIPS
- If your dog runs round the wall, put him back in the Sit. Stand as close to the wall as possible on the other side. Facing your dog, encourage him over using his lead and tidbits.
- If your dog refuses the wall, revert to hurdle training until he displays more confidence (see page 33).
- If your dog fails to clear the wall or lands on it, reduce the height. If he still has problems, place a full-height hurdle immediately before the wall. Only remove the hurdle when your dog is clearing wall and hurdle consistently.
- Practise with him on both sides of you, at both walking and running pace.

SPREAD JUMP
The spread jump consists of two hurdles, of differing heights, joined together to form a double spread. The maximum distance of the whole jump is 2 ft 6 in (76.2 cm) for standard, 1 ft 8 in (50.8 cm) for midi dogs, and 1 ft 3 in (38.1 cm) for mini dogs. The crossbar of the front hurdle should be 6 in (15.2 cm) lower than the rear.

PHASE ONE
- Place two hurdles close together, so that the crossbars are about 15 in (38.1 cm) apart.
- Adjust the height of the cross-bars, so that the front hurdle is set to its lowest height, and the rear hurdle is set 6 in (15.2 cm) higher.
- With your dog on his lead, tell him to Sit facing the jump.
- Command your dog to Wait, and walk round to the other side of the jump. Make sure the lead trails freely over the spread.
- Recall your dog and say "Over" as he jumps.
- Reward his success.

PHASE TWO
- Remove your dog's lead and tell him to sit a few steps away from the jump.
- Walk with your dog towards the jump.
- When you reach it, say "Over" and encourage your dog to jump straight from his last

walking step.
- When he lands the other side, walk him forwards for a few more paces before you reward him.
- Once he is confident, increase the height and breadth of the spread jump until it reaches its maximum extension. Also increase the speed of your dog's pace.
- If he fails, reduce the height and only increase it when he is jumping each level comfortably and confidently.

WATER JUMP

The water jump comprises a hurdle/wall/brush fence, with a trough of water behind it. The spread of the obstacle covers an area of 5 ft (1.52 m) for standard dogs and 3 ft 4 in (1.01 m) for midis and 2 ft 6 in (76 cm) minis. The height of the hurdle is a maximum of 2 ft (60.9 cm) for standard dogs, 1 ft 8 in (50.8 cm) for midis, and 1 ft 3 in (38.1 cm) for minis. This obstacle is rarely seen in Agility competition, because it is far less portable than the other equipment.

Training for the water jump follows the same format as for the spread jump. Some dogs may be intimidated by the water feature, but this is a matter of building up familiarity and confidence. Your biggest problem may be persuading your dog to jump *over* the water, rather than *into* it – a common complaint about water-loving breeds such as the Golden Retriever.

5 Pipes, Pauses and Poles

Most Agility equipment can be classed as jumps or contact obstacles, but a few pieces do not fall into either category. These are the tunnels, the table, the pause box, and the weaving poles.

TUNNELS

There are two types of tunnels: the rigid/pipe tunnel and the collapsible tunnel. Even if you are unfamiliar with other Agility equipment, tunnels are relatively easy to master, and they help to develop the bond between dog and handler. Indeed, some instructors start a dog's training with the tunnel.

PIPE TUNNEL

The tunnel takes its name from its appearance. It is a cylindrical tunnel, held open by a series of hoops attached to its plastic fabric, which allows the dog to pass through without restriction. The

diameter of the tunnel should be no less than 2 ft (60.9 cm).

The tunnel can be compressed or extended like a concertina, enabling it to be set to a variety of different lengths. *The Kennel Club Year Book* states a minimum length of 10 ft (3.05 m).

When training this exercise, it helps to have a friend holding the tunnel to prevent it from rolling. Alternatively, you may anchor the tunnel using tent pegs. Always make sure that your training instructor is present.

PHASE ONE
- Compress the tunnel to its shortest length.
- With your dog attached to a training lead, show him the tunnel. Allow him to sniff and explore it.
- Command your dog to Sit and Wait, at the tunnel entrance. Your instructor

THE RIGID TUNNEL

The rigid/pipe tunnel is compressed to its shortest length. The instructor holds the dog at one end of the tunnel, allowing a clear view of the handler on the other side, who is holding the lead.

The dog is called through the tunnel.

should hold your dog so that he is pointing at the tunnel entrance.

- Trail the lead through the tunnel, and hold it at the other end of the tunnel to your dog. Make sure that your dog can see you clearly through the tunnel.
- Recall your dog.
- Reward him when he comes. If he fails to respond, pull gently on your dog's lead to encourage him to come to you, and increase the reward, giving more tidbits or praise, for example.
- Once he is confident, repeat the exercise off-lead.

PHASE TWO

- Stand a few steps away from the tunnel, with your dog sitting by your side.
- Walk forward with your dog, and encourage him to go through the tunnel. Ask your friend to crouch at the other end with a reward/toy as a lure.
- As he goes through, call "Tunnel", and run towards the other end.
- As soon as your dog emerges, reward him.

- Gradually extend the tunnel and the speed with which your dog runs through it.

PHASE THREE

- Compress the tunnel to half its length and create a slight bend halfway along.
- Command your dog to Sit and Wait a few steps away from the tunnel.
- Walk to the tunnel and command your dog "Tunnel", making him go through the entrance.
- At this stage, your dog should walk straight into the tunnel without stopping. He should be confident, despite the fact that the bend is preventing him from seeing daylight (if he is not, return to phases one and two).
- As your dog moves through the tunnel, keep abreast him on the outside, and reassure him that you are near.
- Reward him when he arrives at the other end.
- Gradually increase the length of the tunnel and the angle of the bend. Eventually, your dog should be confident enough to tackle a U-shaped bend in a full-length tunnel.

Above: The tunnel is compressed to half-length with a slight bend. The dog is commanded "Tunnel"/"Through".

Left: The dog runs confidently through the tunnel and emerges at the other end.

PHASE FOUR
- Set the tunnel to its full length, then walk away from it, accompanied by your dog.
- Turn around and run towards the tunnel, again with your dog at your side.
- Command "Tunnel", and encourage your dog to go on through the tunnel without waiting at the entrance first.
- When he emerges at the other end, run with him for a few paces before stopping him to give him his reward.

COLLAPSIBLE TUNNEL
The Kennel Club Year Book defines the collapsible tunnel as *"circular, of non-rigid construction"*. The tunnel, which must be a minimum of 10 ft (3.05 m), is usually made of cloth. It is held open at one end by a separate entrance piece, which must have a minimum diameter of 19 in (48.3 cm). The Kennel Club requires the entrance piece to have a non-slip floor, a padded surround, and to be anchored securely to the ground. The dog enters the tunnel through the open entrance, and then has to push his way through the folds of cloth until he emerges at the other end.

When your dog is inside the tunnel, he will be unable to see where he going. Many dogs find this unnerving, and yours should trust you completely before attempting this obstacle. Only train with your instructor.

PHASE ONE
- Fold the cloth of the tunnel right back, so that the tunnel is no longer than its separate entrance piece.
- Sit your dog so that he is facing the entrance with your instructor holding him.
- Walk to the other side of the tunnel, hold the cloth open and then call your dog through.
- As he runs through, say "Tunnel".
- Reward him when he finishes.
- Gradually extend the tunnel to 5 ft (1.52 m), with the instructor still holding him, and you holding open the canvas end so that your dog can still see daylight.

PHASE TWO
- Ask your instructor to go to

THE COLLAPSIBLE TUNNEL

◄ *The cloth of the collapsible tunnel is folded back.*

The tunnel entrance is held open, and the handler calls the dog through. ►

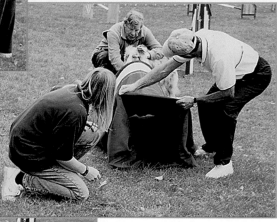

◄ *Instant reward is given as the dog emerges.*

the cloth end of the tunnel and hold it open.

- With the tunnel at half-length, call your dog through.
- When your dog is halfway through, get your instructor to lower the canvas slightly so that it brushes your dog's back. Do not lower the cloth so much that your dog is plunged into darkness.
- Repeat this several times, until your dog becomes used to the feel of the canvas against him.
- Gradually increase the drop of the canvas, until your dog is running through the tunnel in darkness.
- Once he is confident, extend the tunnel, in stages, to its maximum length.
- Reward each success.

PHASE THREE

- Instead of commanding your dog to Sit and Wait at the tunnel entrance, position yourself a few paces away.
- With your dog by your side, walk towards the tunnel.
- When you reach the entrance, do not stop. Instead, command "Tunnel", give the hand signal (see page 31), and encourage your dog to go

straight in.

- While your dog runs the length of the tunnel, run to the other end.
- When your dog emerges, do not let him stop. Instead, run for a few paces before rewarding him.

PAUSE OBSTACLES

Any dog competing in Agility is obviously full of energy and enthusiasm. To test how much control you, the handler, have over those qualities, some Agility courses contain a pause box or table. The dog has to position himself in or on the obstacle, and lie down for five seconds. It may sound easy, but pause obstacles can be very tricky – lying down is the last thing most dogs want to do when in full flow!

PAUSE BOX

KC-approved pause boxes measure 4 ft² (1.22 m²). The box is on the ground.

PHASE ONE

- Position your dog in the pause box and stand next to him.
- Command him to go Down,

Position your dog a few paces from the tunnel.

Give the command "Tunnel"/"Through".

Allow the dog to run on for a couple of paces before rewarding him.

THE PAUSE BOX

The dog is commanded to go into the pause box.

The dog heads for the pause box. A toy can be placed in the box as a lure.

On command, the dog goes into the Down.

The dog is commanded to Wait, and must stay in position for five seconds.

and give your hand signal (see page 28).

- Reward him when he obeys.
- Command him to Wait, and count to five, starting from one.
- Reward him for staying in the Down position.
- Give the release command and encourage your dog to move from the pause box to the next obstacle.
- Reward him.
- Repeat and reduce the rewards, until you are rewarding your dog only after he has completed the whole sequence.
- Practise until perfect, and then introduce distractions. Remember that your dog must do this in the presence of lots of people and lots of background noise.

PHASE TWO

- With your dog, stand a few steps away from the pause box.
- Walk with your dog towards the pause box and command your dog to go Down as soon as he reaches the middle of the box.
- Command him to Wait.

- After five seconds, say "Off" and move away with your dog, rewarding him once you are a step or two away from the pause box.
- Repeat, at a run.
- Gradually extend the distance between you and your dog, so that he will Down on command at a distance of a few metres. Use the five-second Down to catch up. This will enable you to move away together.

PHASE THREE

- With your instructor and a reward toy in the pause box, send your dog forward to the obstacle.
- Your instructor should help your dog to achieve the Down position.
- Continue practising, until your dog is able to complete the exercise confidently and without the instructor's help.

TABLE

The table is slightly smaller than the pause box, measuring 3 ft^2 (94.1 cm^2). It is raised off the ground to a height dictated by the dog's size: 2 ft 6 in/76.2 cm for standard; 1 ft 8 in/50.8 cm

The table exercise should be taught after the dog has mastered the pause box.

for midi; 15 in/38.1 cm for mini. It must have a non-slip surface so that the dog does not slip and hurt himself.

The dog must run to the table, jump on to its surface, Down for five seconds, then jump off and move away with his handler. Teach the table exercise after teaching the pause box exercise.

PHASE ONE

- Place the table top on the ground, so that there is only the thickness of the table top in height.

- Stand next to your dog on the table top.
- Command "Down" and give your hand signal (see page 28).
- Reward him.
- Command him to Wait.
- Reward.
- Command "Off" and move with your dog from the table top.
- Gradually extend the Wait to the full five seconds.
- Raise the height of the table, in stages, so that the dog has to jump off from a height.

PHASE TWO

- Position the table at ground level.
- Sit your dog two paces away from the table.
- Walk with him towards the table.
- Command "Table" as he reaches it, give your hand signal, and encourage him to walk on to the table top.
- Reward him instantly.
- Repeat, gradually raising the height of the table so that your dog has to jump on to it.

PHASE THREE

- Repeat phase two, but as soon as your dog is on the table top, command him "Down" and give your hand signal.
- Reward him instantly when he goes Down, then command "Wait".
- Command "Off", and walk a few steps away before rewarding.
- Gradually build up the Wait to the full five seconds.
- Practise the full sequence, rewarding your dog only once he has successfully completed the whole sequence.
- As with the pause box, practise your Sendaway so that your dog jumps on the table ahead of you. Increase the distance gradually.
- When he jumps on the table and Downs at a distance, you will be able to increase the speed of your course.

WEAVING POLES

During this exercise, the dog must weave his way through a line of poles positioned in the

Weaving poles designed with a wired, confined channel for training purposes.

The handler walks alongside the weaving poles, and the dog is on the inside.

ground. The number of poles is determined by the judge, from five up to twelve. The minimum distance between the poles is 18 in (45.7 cm), and the maximum is 24 in (60.9 cm). The poles must be of rigid construction, 2 ft 6 in (76.2 cm) tall, and 3/4-2 in (1.9-3.8 cm) in diameter.

The dog has to begin the weave with the first pole adjacent to his left side. Tackling the poles from his right side incurs a penalty. Failure to complete the course correctly will result in elimination, so it is important to ensure that you teach this correctly.

While there are several ways to train the weave, we prefer the wired, confined-channel method (above). Your training club should have a confined-channel training frame on which you can practise.

PHASE ONE

- Set the frame so that the channel is approximately 18 in (45 cm) wide.
- With your dog on a short training lead, command "Weave", give your hand signal (see page 31), and have your dog enter the training frame so that it is positioned on his left.
- Walk with your dog inside, and you outside, the channel. Ensure that he does not jump out. As he walks, repeat "Weave" excitedly.

- Reward him for his success.
- Repeat several times, until your dog is familiar with the voice command and the hand signal for Weave.

PHASE TWO
- Place your dog in a Sit at the entrance of the training frame, so that it is positioned to his left.
- Command "Wait" while you walk to the other end of the frame.
- Command "Weave" and Recall your dog to you.
- Reward him for his success.

PHASE THREE
- Position your dog off-lead in a Sit, so that the frame entrance is slightly to his left.
- Throw a favourite toy along the length of the frame, so that it lands just beyond the exit. Command "Weave" as you do this, and encourage your dog to chase after the toy. Alternatively, have your instructor, standing at the other end of the poles, show the toy/treat to your dog.
- As your dog runs down the channel, run alongside him. Make sure that your voice

and body language are encouraging.
- At the end, reward your dog with a game involving his toy/tidbit.
- Repeat regularly, slowly reducing the width of the channel. Do not rush this stage, or your dog's confidence and accuracy could be forfeited.

PHASE FOUR
- Set up the frame so that one of the middle wires is removed.
- Walk your dog down the adjusted channel, not forgetting to say "Weave" and to give your hand signal.
- Reward him.
- Keep practising, and after every four or five successful runs, remove another wire.
- Repeat until your dog is able to run the length of the training frame without any of the guiding wires.

PHASE FIVE
- Position yourself and your dog a few steps away from the frame.
- Walk slowly towards the frame, and encourage the dog to enter without stopping

TEACHING WEAVING

Above left: The instructor holds the dog at the start of the weaving poles.

Above right: The handler calls the dog forward.

Left: At the end of the weaving poles the dog is rewarded.

Above left: A ball or a food treat can be used as an incentive.

Above right: The handler runs alongside the weaving poles with the dog on the lead.

Right: As the ball is thrown, the lead is dropped, and the dog gets his reward.

The dog is now ready to move on to weaving poles. To begin with, they are staggered to make it easier.

first. Make sure he enters with the first pole on his left side.

- Reward him at the other end.
- Practise until your dog can do the exercise at a running pace.
- By now, your dog should be tackling the weave on voice command and hand signal alone. Train him to attempt the weave while you are a few steps behind him, rather than adjacent to him.

PHASE SIX

- Replace the training frame with the proper weaving poles.
- Practise the complete weave, rewarding each successful attempt.
- Alternate between an odd number and an even number of poles.
- Make sure you run on either side of your dog.
- Add a hurdle at the far end of the poles, on either side, so that your dog learns to exit the weave in a straight, correct manner.
- Once your dog has become proficient at the weave, take every opportunity to practise on the weaving poles of other clubs. They may look similar to you, but they do not to your dog!

The weaving poles are now straight and the dog tackles them with complete confidence.

Advanced jumps include the long jump, the tyre/hoop, and the wishing well/lych gate. These jumps are more difficult than the basic hurdles because a greater degree of accuracy is required, particularly if the dog is of a larger breed.

LONG JUMP

The long jump consists of a front hurdle and a rear hurdle, with a number of elements. These are arranged so that the dog must clear the whole lot in one go. The elements are raised off the ground, with the emphasis on distance rather than height. The maximum height for the front element is 5 in (12.7 cm), for dogs of every size. The last is adjusted according to the size of the dog: 15 in (38.1 cm) for standard, 12 in (30.5 cm) for

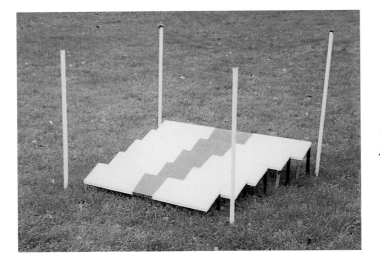

The elements of the long jump.

midi, and 9 in (22.8 cm) for mini.

There are three to five units, and the number of the units also determines the length of the long jump. This is 5 ft (1.52 m) for standard dogs, 3 ft 4 in (10.16 cm) for midi, and 2 ft 6 in (76.2 cm) for mini.

PHASE ONE

- Set the long jump so that it consists of two units placed next to each other.
- With your dog on his training lead, put him in a Sit facing the jump.
- Command him to Wait, and walk round to the other side of the hurdles, trailing the lead over the jump.
- Call him to you using the Recall (see page 27).
- Reward him when he jumps.
- If your dog fails to jump, use his lead to encourage him over the obstacle.
- Move the units a little further apart, and repeat the exercise.

PHASE TWO

- Depending on the dog's size, set up three units.
- Sit your dog on one side of the jump, and face him on the other.
- Ask him to jump, and reward him when he does so.
- When he is confident, increase the number of elements until your dog is confidently tackling the long jump at maximum extension for his size.

PHASE THREE

- Reduce the length of the long jump so that your dog can jump it with minimum effort.
- Remove his lead and command him to Sit so that he is facing the obstacle. Stand by his right side.
- Walk towards the long jump.
- When you reach the jump, command your dog "Over" and give your hand signal (see page 30).
- Reward him when he succeeds.
- Repeat with your dog on your other side.

PHASE FOUR

- Set the long jump to a short distance.
- With your dog off-lead, ask him to Sit facing the jump.
- Together, run towards the long jump.
- When your dog reaches the jump, command him "Over"

THE LONG JUMP

Start with two units of the long jump. The dog, on lead, is placed in the Sit.

The handler calls the dog through.

The handler stands facing the dog who is now off-lead.

The dogs shows a swift response to the Recall.

Confidence, built up over many training sessions, is the key to leaping the long jump (now at its full extent) with ease.

with your voice command and hand signal.
- Reward success.
- Repeat, until your dog is jumping confidently on either side of you at a run.
- Gradually extend the distance of the jump and the speed at which your dog tackles it.

PROBLEMS
Most problems with the long jump are the result of a lack of confidence on the dog's part. Never push too far too quickly.

TYRE/HOOP
These obstacles consist of a raised, circular opening of a tyre or plastic hoop, through which the dog must jump. The obstacle is raised off the ground, using one of two different methods.
- The tyre/hoop is attached to the top of a pole which is adjusted to the appropriate height.
- The tyre/hoop is suspended from a frame by a series of chains or springs.

Ensure that you practise using a hoop and a tyre, and both methods of mounting. Remember that they look very different to your dog.

Whichever method of mounting is used, the entire obstacle must be securely anchored to the ground, so that it cannot be knocked over by the dog. Any chains present in a frame-mounted tyre should be covered with a suitable padding material.

The height of the centre of the obstacle is 3 ft (91.4 cm) from the ground for standard dogs. For midi dogs the height is reduced to 2 ft (60.9 cm), while for mini dogs it is reduced further, to 1 ft 8 in (50.8 cm). Most dogs will jump this height easily; it is the diameter of the aperture – 18 in (45.7 cm) – which makes the obstacle challenging, particularly for bigger dogs.

Before beginning training for this obstacle, all the hurdle jumps should be mastered. It also helps to have tackled the tunnels.

PHASE ONE
- Ask a friend or your instructor to hold the tyre vertically. At this stage, do not raise it off the ground.
- With your dog on a loose training lead, command him to Sit and Wait. Ask your instructor to pass the lead through the tyre.

THE TYRE

The 'lollipop' tyre is set at its lowest height. The dog, on a lead, is in the Sit, with the handler facing.

The dog is called through.

The second type of tyre, suspended from a frame, is taught in exactly the same way as the lollipop tyre.

- Go to the other side of the tyre, turn to face your dog, and kneel down so that your face is framed by the tyre.
- Recall your dog, using the lead to encourage him through the tyre if necessary.
- As he comes through, say "Tyre".
- Reward him once he reaches you.

PHASE TWO

- Set up the tyre as in phase one.
- Ask your dog to Sit facing the tyre. Stand by his side.
- Using the voice command and hand signal for this piece of equipment (see page 32), encourage your dog through.
- Walk around the tyre to meet him at the other side.
- Reward him on completion.
- Practise, alternating the side which you are on, and gradually raising the height of the tyre.

PHASE THREE

- Reset the tyre so that it is touching the ground.
- Position your dog several paces away from the tyre, and stand by his side.

- Walk towards the tyre with your dog, saying "Tyre" as soon as you reach it.
- Encourage your dog to go through the tyre from a short walk-up, without stopping first. If he refuses, or goes round, throw a toy/lure through the aperture.
- Do not forget to reward his success.
- Repeat, increasing your dog's speed until he can tackle the obstacle on the run.
- Once your dog is fast and confident, gradually raise the height of the tyre.

WISHING WELL/LYCH GATE

This obstacle takes its name from its appearance. It consists of a hurdle with a roof, and the dog must jump through the gap between the two. For this reason, this jump should not be taught until your dog has

The wishing well should not be attempted until the dog is proficient over ordinary hurdles.

mastered the hurdle, the tyre and the spread jump.

The wishing well is a minimum of 2 ft 8 in (81.3 cm) wide, which, for larger dogs, makes it slightly easier than the tyre. The minimum gap between the crossbar and the roof is 30 in (76.2 cm), although this can be increased. The roof should be a minimum of 5 ft (1.52 m) from the ground, while the crossbar has a height limit which is adjustable according to the size of the dog: 2 ft 6 in (76.2 cm) for standard, 1 ft 8 in (50.8 cm) for midi, and 1 ft 3 in (38.1 cm) for mini. The dog is faulted if he dislodges the crossbar, or if he touches the base.

PHASE ONE

- Set up the wishing well so that the crossbar is at its minimum height.
- Attach a training lead to your dog, and ask him to Sit and Wait so he is facing the jump.
- Feeding the lead through the gap between the crossbar and the roof, walk to the other side of the jump and turn to face your dog.

- Command "Over", along with your hand signal (see page 30), and encourage your dog to jump through the gap. Use the lead and a lure to encourage him through the gap.
- Praise and reward.
- Once your dog understands what is required of him, remove the training lead.
- Continue practising, and slowly raise the height of the crossbar.

PHASE TWO

- Set up the obstacle so that the crossbar is at its lowest height.
- With your dog by your side, position yourself a few paces away from the wishing well, and turn to face it.
- Walk towards the jump and encourage your dog to jump it straight from a walking pace.
- Reward him if he is successful.
- Increase speed, until your dog is able to jump the wishing well from a running pace. Do not forget to run on alternate sides.
- As your dog's confidence increases, gradually raise the height of the crossbar.

PHASE THREE

- Place a basic hurdle approximately 16-20 ft (5-6 m) from the wishing well.
- Repeat the above, but this time make your dog jump the wishing well and the hurdle. This will accustom him to tackling obstacle after obstacle in sequence.

TIPS

- If your dog steps on the well, do not reprimand him – it seems sensible to him. Instead, ask your instructor to hold another pole just above the base.
- If your dog attempts to jump the roof, remove it. Replace it only once your dog is jumping confidently.

7 Contact Obstacles

There are four contact obstacles on an Agility course. They are the A-ramp, the dog-walk, the see-saw, and the cross-over (the last of the four being seldom used). Contact equipment is so called because each obstacle has certain areas at the beginning and end, which the dog must touch with his feet.

To teach the contact obstacles, you must first teach your dog about contact points. Begin with contact training, familiarising your dog with the contact points on each individual obstacle, *before* you tackle the whole obstacle in one go.

In the heat of a competition, it is all too easy to miss the contact points.

CONTACT TRAINING

As well as a method that can be used to begin instruction, contact training can be used throughout all stages of contact-obstacle tutoring.

Competitors often find that their dogs achieve all the contacts in training, but miss them when competing. This is largely an effect of the competition environment, where there are more distractions and a decrease in concentration. Improved speed can also contribute to the problem.

Specialised contact training helps to overcome the problem. If your dog begins to miss the contacts in training or competition, it is also helpful to revert to contact training methods once again. As an extra tip, also try incorporating distractions into your training sessions. Your dog will then build up an increased resistance during competition.

HOOP METHOD

Your club should have a training hoop, but you can also make your own using some plastic tubing. For a Collie-sized dog, you will need a length of approximately 6 ft (1.8 m). Join the ends together to form a hoop, and insert some wooden dowel rods to give the tubing more firmness and shape. Alternatively, a slim tyre of the correct size is equally suitable.

PHASE ONE
- Have your instructor or a friend hold the hoop upright, with its base on the ground.
- Place a plank through the hoop for your dog to walk on.
- Ask your dog to Sit and Wait so he is facing the hoop.
- Go to the other side of the hoop and call your dog to you.
- Reward him for his success.
- Repeat the exercise, this time *sending* your dog through, rather than recalling him.

PHASE TWO
- Place a hoop at the beginning and at the end of each contact obstacle.
- Send your dog through the starting hoop, and reward quickly.
- Do not let your dog stop. Instead, instruct him to carry on.
- When he reaches the end of the obstacle, send your dog

HOOP METHOD

The hoop is used to focus the dog, slowing him down for the contact.

The hoop should only be removed once it is second nature to your dog to touch all the contact points.

through the second hoop.
- Reward.
- Repeat until your dog is consistently touching the contact points, at which time the hoops can be removed.

DOWN METHOD

Before you can use this method, your dog should be able to produce an instant Down, Sit or Stand, on command. This technique can be used on its own, or in conjunction with the hoop or lure methods. You will need a plank of wood when practising.

PHASE ONE

- Place your training plank on the ground, and position your dog at one end.
- Command him to Walk On, then, as soon as he has all four paws on the plank, command him Down with your hand signal (see page 28).
- Reward and repeat.
- Add an instant Down at the far end of the plank, before commanding "Off".
- Command your dog Down with a hand signal, as soon as he steps off the plank at the far end.

- Repeat, alternating the side on which you stand.

PHASE TWO

- Incorporate instant Downs on all the contact points for the obstacle being taught.
- Reward each correct response.
- Practise until the rewards can be withdrawn.
- Gradually remove the Downs, once your dog is performing his manoeuvres correctly.
- Use them randomly thereafter.

LURE METHOD

For this method, you will need a plentiful supply of treats or a favourite toy. You may also use a clicker-training device as a reward. When a dog is so trained, you can dispense with tidbits, except at random.

PHASE ONE

- Position your dog at the start of the plank, and use the lure to guide him on.
- Reward the correct response with the treat or a click. If using a toy, do not let your dog play with the toy as this will distract him and interrupt training.
- Repeat several times.

- Place the lure about 3 in (7 cm) from the end of your training plank.
- Send your dog up the plank, encouraging him to find the lure.
- Repeat several times.

PHASE TWO

- Use the lure to encourage your dog on and off each contact obstacle, and to make sure that he makes contact with the relevant points.
- Repeat, gradually withdrawing the lure and rewards, until your dog is tackling each obstacle correctly on voice command and hand signal alone.

A-RAMP

This obstacle consists of two 3 ft-wide (0.91 m), 9 ft-long (2.74 m) boards, joined together at the apex with a hinge mechanism. The hinge allows the whole obstacle to be placed either flat on the ground, or erected in the shape of an 'A' of varying gradient. At its steepest, the A-ramp is 6 ft 3 in (1.91 m) high. There are slats on the ramp to assist your dog's grip in this exercise.

To complete the A-ramp successfully, your dog must run up one side of the frame, go over the top, and run down the other side, making contact with the designated areas on each side. The contact points are the bottom-most 3 ft 6 in (1.07 m) of each side of the ramp. These areas are marked in a different colour.

Your dog will be penalised if he fails to touch the contact areas. The points are not only a test of control and training, but are there to prevent your dog from hurting himself. Some dogs, particularly the larger breeds, may cause serious damage to their joints and ligaments if they leave the A-ramp from too great a height.

Although it appears daunting, the A-ramp is one of the easier obstacles to learn. There are four training methods, all of which are equally suitable. When training, the ramp should be erected at near its full height. Some people prefer it to be almost flat, but this is not necessary.

PLACING METHOD

The placing method is a gentle and gradual way to accustom your dog to the A-ramp.

PHASE ONE

- Erect the A-ramp.
- Attach a training lead to your dog and lift him on to the contact area of the down ramp.
- Command him to Wait, and hold him there for a few seconds.
- Release him by saying "Off" going downwards. Reward him.
- Repeat, on both sides of the ramp, until your dog is confident.
- Gradually extend the length of time which your dog must wait.
- Once he seems confident, repeat the exercise, gradually positioning your dog nearer to the apex, but still facing downwards.

PHASE TWO

- Position your dog a few paces away from the A-ramp.
- With you standing on one side, and your instructor on the other, walk your dog towards the ramp.
- When you reach the ramp, say "Walk On", and walk your dog up the ramp. Ensure he touches the up contact.

- Walk your dog over the apex and down the other side.
- Stop half-way down and command your dog to Wait for a few seconds.
- Continue to walk down the ramp, giving the "Off" command at the end.
- Reward your dog.
- Repeat until your dog is confident, then incorporate a Wait on the up ramp.

PHASE THREE

- Repeat phase two, but remain on the ground with only your dog on the A-ramp.
- Once he is confident, increase speed.

RECALL METHOD

- Erect the A-ramp.
- Attach a training lead to your dog, and ask him to Sit and Wait so that he is facing the ramp, approximately 10 ft (3 m) from the base. Ask your instructor to hold him in position.
- Walk round to the other side of the obstacle, and climb it until you reach the apex. Leave space for your dog to pass you on the ramp.
- Call your dog to you using the

THE A-RAMP

Above: For novice dogs, the A-ramp should be at its widest spread.

Left: Initially, the dog is held on the contact and rewarded.

Recall and a reward as a lure.

- As your dog comes up towards you, say "Ramp", and throw his lure down the other side of the obstacle. Your instructor can help by running by the side of the ramp with your dog, holding on to the training lead to ensure that the dog does not leave the down ramp too early.

- Reward your dog once he completes the run.

- Repeat, until your dog can tackle the ramp without assistance.

Left: In the next stage, the dog is placed higher up the ramp.

Right: The handler and instructor guide the dog down the ramp.

Left: Pause and reward on the contact.

Some dogs need more encouragement. Here, the handler has climbed up the ramp, and is holding a ball as a lure.

Guided by the instructor, the dog goes up the ramp and is rewarded by getting the ball.

The dog is ready to tackle the A-ramp (now at full height) off-lead.

In training, a reward is still given on the contact.

RUNNING METHOD

- Erect the A-ramp.
- Command your dog to Sit facing the up ramp. You stand on one side, and your instructor stands on the other. Each of you holds a finger in his collar. Two short leads may also be used.
- Say "Ramp", give your hand signal (see page 30), and run towards the obstacle, accompanied by your instructor and your dog.
- When you reach the ramp, you and your instructor should continue to run each side on the ground, while your dog will run up the A-ramp and down the other side. Leave his collar when the appropriate height is reached.
- Reward once your dog completes the run.
- Practise until your dog is confident and the instructor is no longer needed.

INSTRUCTOR METHOD

- Erect the A-ramp, and have your instructor balance on the apex.
- With your dog on a short training lead, run him up the ramp. You should remain on the ground.
- When you cannot reach any further, hand your dog's lead over to the instructor, who will help your dog tackle the apex and begin his descent on the other side.
- Run around to the other side of the ramp, and reclaim the lead from your instructor.
- Run your dog down and off the down ramp.
- Repeat, this time incorporating your voice command, "Ramp", and the appropriate hand signal (see page 30).
- Practise until your dog is performing consistently and confidently.

DOG-WALK

This consists of a narrow plank, raised 4 ft 6 in (1.37 m) from the ground, with a ramp at the beginning and end. The dog has to run up one ramp, across the walkway, and down the other ramp.

The planks are 10-12 in (25.4-30.5 cm) wide, and the complete walkway is 12-14 ft (3.66-4.27 m) long. The groundmost 3 ft (91.4 cm) of the up/down ramps are a different colour, indicating the area with which the dog should make contact. Each ramp should be of a non-slip material, with anti-slip slats at intervals. If the dog fails to make contact with the designated areas, he is faulted.

PLACING METHOD

This method is the same as that used to teach the A-ramp.

PHASE ONE

- Take the main part of the dog-walk and lie it flat on the ground. Enclose it with a wire frame (as for the weaving poles).
- With your dog on his training lead, walk him along the plank.
- Reward your dog and repeat the exercise until he is confident.

PHASE TWO

- With your dog on a lead, walk him along the training plank, and, shortly before the end, command him to Wait.
- After a few seconds, continue walking.
- When you reach the end, say "Off", and walk your dog off the end.
- Reward and repeat.

PHASE THREE

- Walk along the training plank as before.
- A few paces from the far end, command your dog to Stand and Wait.
- Walk to the end and call your dog to you.
- As he disembarks, command him "Off".
- Repeat, making sure you walk on alternate sides of the obstacle.
- Reward.

PHASE FOUR

- Position your dog a few steps away from the beginning of the dog-walk.
- Walk him forward, this time without his lead, saying "Walk on" and giving your hand signal (see page 30) when you reach the up plank.
- Encourage your dog to walk on to the ramp without pausing.
- After a few steps forward, command him to Stand and Wait for a few seconds.
- Release him from the Wait, reward him, and ask him to continue forwards.
- Command him to Wait shortly before the end.
- Release him and reward him.

THE DOG-WALK

Above left: The dog is placed on the contact of the dog-walk.

Above right: The handler goes to the end of the lead.

Left: The dog is called down through the contact.

- Command him "Off", and let him walk off the end of the dog-walk.
- Reward and repeat.

PHASE FIVE

- Combine all the elements, so that your dog walks the length of the obstacle in one movement, and touches all the contact points.
- Practise, until your dog understands exactly what is required and can carry out the exercise with the vocal commands and hand signals alone.
- Repeat, making sure that you practise mounting the walk from the two different ends.
- Gradually increase the dog's speed, and the height of the dog-walk.

WALK ON/RUN METHOD

If you are new to Agility, we recommend that you try the placing method before progressing to the walk on/run method.

PHASE ONE

- Build the dog-walk to its full height.

- Position your dog, on his lead, between you and your instructor. You should all face the up ramp of the dog-walk.
- In parallel, walk towards the up ramp.
- When you reach it, say "Walk On" and encourage your dog up the ramp.
- Put your hand on your dog's collar if he struggles, and encourage him forwards with a toy or other reward.
- Continue to walk the length of the plank, and down the other side, saying "Off" just before he jumps off.
- Practise until your dog is confident.

PHASE TWO

- Remove the lead and repeat phase one.
- As you say "Walk On", introduce your hand signal also (see page 30).
- Do not forget to walk on alternate sides of your dog.
- Include your chosen method of contact training (see page 70).
- Build up the dog's speed.

The dog is lifted higher up the dog-walk.

The handler and instructor guide the dog.

The dog is called down through the contact.

Left: Off-lead, the dog runs up the dog-walk and maintains a steady pace along the top.

Bottom left: Heading down the ramp.

Bottom right: A good contact as the dog heads off the dog-walk.

SEE-SAW

Much like its playground equivalent, the see-saw is a narrow plank, 10-12 in (25.4-30.5 cm) wide, which is balanced on a central fulcrum, which may be up to 2 ft 3 in (68.5 cm) high. The dog has to walk the length of the see-saw, a distance of 12-14 ft (13.66-4.27 m), starting by walking on to the lowered end. He then has to progress to the centre, and tip the see-saw – without losing his balance – to make the far end touch the ground. Then he must walk down the remaining plank and touch the contact area before disembarking.

The contact areas of this obstacle are the furthermost 3 ft (91.4 cm) of each end of the see-saw. They are painted in a different colour. If the dog fails to make contact with these areas, then he's penalised accordingly.

As with the other contact obstacles, the see-saw should be made of a non-slip material. These are particularly important since your dog's balance will be tested when he tips the see-saw. You should only attempt this obstacle after your dog has tackled the A-ramp and the dog-walk, and it is more important than ever to enlist the help of a qualified instructor.

PHASE ONE

- With your dog on a short training lead, position him between you and your instructor, so that you are all facing the start of the see-saw. You should be approximately 6 ft (1.8 m) away from the see-saw.
- In parallel, walk towards the see-saw.
- When you reach it, do not stop. Simply walk your dog up the see-saw with a minimum of fuss – give him the impression that you are totally relaxed and that there is nothing unusual about walking up a narrow plank.
- Hold a tidbit in your hand and position it just in front of the dog's nose. Use it to lure your dog forwards along the see-saw.
- Pause at the pivot point, and command your dog to Wait.
- Slowly guide your dog forwards, so that he tips the see-saw. Get your instructor to control the tilt, making sure it is gradual so as not to

The dog is held on the see-saw contact point.

frighten the dog.

- Reward, then continue forwards.
- Walk your dog to the end of the see-saw, commanding him "Off" at the end.
- Reward and repeat until confident.

PHASE TWO

- Repeat phase one, but remove your dog's lead.
- Once confident, repeat the exercise but without your instructor walking in parallel with you and your dog (but still controlling the tilt of the see-saw).
- Repeat, this time without the instructor controlling the pivotal point.

PHASE THREE

- Set up the see-saw.
- Position your dog in a Sit, several steps away from the apparatus.
- Give your hand signal (see page 30), and command your dog to Walk On, moving towards the see-saw and straight on to it.
- Do not stop, but continue the whole length of the see-saw, making sure that your dog touches both contact areas before you command him "Off".

THE SEE-SAW

1. With the see-saw sloping down, the dog is placed on the pivot.

2. The see-saw is now allowed to tilt.

3. The dog is walked down to the contact.

4. Pause and reward on the contact.

Tackling the see-saw off-lead.

- Continue to walk forwards for a few steps before you reward your dog.
- Repeat, making sure that you approach the obstacle from both ends.
- Gradually increase your dog's speed.

CROSS-OVER

The cross-over consists of a square table with four planks securely attached to it which act as ramps. The dog has to travel up one of the planks, move across the table to the plank chosen by the judge, and then walk down that ramp, touching the contact points on his way up and down.

The table itself is 4 ft (1.22 m) high, and 2 ft 8 in (81.8 cm) square on the top. Each of the planks is 10 in (25.4 cm) wide, and 12 ft (3.66 m) long. The end 3 ft (91.4 cm) of each plank is a different colour to indicate the area with which the dog should make contact. Each ramp has anti-slip slats.

The cross-over is a less common contact obstacle than the other three. This is mainly because of the difficulty in acquiring such a high table. It is not a particularly difficult obstacle, but should not be tackled until your dog has completed training for the dog-walk.

PHASE ONE

- Set up the cross-over at full height.
- With your dog on a short training lead, walk him up one plank, saying "Walk On", and giving your hand signal (see page 30), as you do so.
- When he is on the table, command him "Steady", but do not let him stop, sit or go down. Ideally, you just want him to slow his pace and pay attention.
- Command your dog straight on, walking him down the opposite plank to the one which he came up. Make sure he touches the contact point.
- Say "Off", and walk your dog off the ramp, then reward.
- Repeat until your dog is confident and appears to understand what is required of him.

PHASE TWO

- Repeat phase one, but, when your dog is steady on the table top, guide him to the left or right plank, using the appropriate vocal command and hand signal (see page 30).
- Repeat until he understands, from the command and signal, the direction in which you want him to go.
- Repeat until your dog is able to tackle the obstacle off-lead.
- Do not forget to reward each successful attempt.

PHASE THREE

- As with the training for the other contact obstacles, progress to sending your dog up the plank without you by his side.
- Stand on different sides of your dog when giving your commands.
- Practise regularly, until your dog is able to complete the cross-over at speed.

8 The Complete Course

Once you and your dog have mastered the individual obstacles, you should learn how to link them together in order to run a whole course. At this point, your dog should be going 'freestyle', which means at high speed, off-lead, and guided only by your instructions.

PUTTING IT TOGETHER

The key to completing an entire round successfully is to combine obstacles. Begin by combining just one or two, and then add more, gradually increasing your speed over each section. Eventually, you will tackle a complete round.

PHASE ONE

- Place two hurdles, one in front of the other.
- Position your dog in a Sit before the first hurdle. Command him to Wait.
- Move to the other side of the first hurdle, and recall your dog.
- Reward.
- Command him to Sit and Wait.
- Move to the other side of the second hurdle and recall him.
- Reward.
- Reposition your dog in a Sit before the first hurdle. Command him to Wait.
- Walk to the far side of the second hurdle and recall your dog.
- If he stops after the first jump, recall him again.
- Reward him only after he has successfully jumped both hurdles in succession.
- Practise regularly.
- Add another hurdle to the sequence, and repeat.
- Do not forget to alternate between running on your dog's left and right sides.

PHASE TWO

- Repeat phase one, but this

PUTTING IT TOGETHER

◄ Dog and handler must work as a team.

Changes of direction must be clearly signalled. ►

◄ Plan ahead, always looking for your next obstacle.

time Sendaway your dog ahead of you, rather than calling him to you. Do not forget to use your hand signal when you give your vocal command.

- Practise on both sides of the hurdles as your dog jumps.

PHASE THREE

- Position two hurdles so that the second is placed at a 45-degree angle to the left of the first.
- Command your dog Over the first hurdle and then instruct him to Wait.
- Move to the side nearest the second hurdle.
- Using voice and hand signals combined (see page 29), command "Back" (for left).
- Command him Over the second hurdle.
- Reward.
- Repeat, this time with the second hurdle at a 45-degree angle to the right of the first, and commanding "Right".
- As your dog increases in confidence, increase the angle until the second hurdle is at 90 degrees to the first.

PHASE FOUR

- Add another hurdle before the first, so that your dog must jump two straight hurdles followed by one at an angle.
- Once he is jumping this confidently, change the hurdles so that the first is straight, the second at an angle to the left, and the third is straight. This requires your dog to run and jump in a zig-zag pattern.
- Reward and repeat until you are both confident.
- Practise the sequence in reverse order, so that your dog has to jump the second hurdle by changing direction to the right.

PHASE FIVE

- Set up a 'mini' training course. For example: two straight hurdles, a tunnel, and two more hurdles.
- Command your dog Over the first two hurdles.
- Reward, then *immediately* instruct him to go through the tunnel.
- Reward and repeat several times.
- Repeat the above, but command your dog Over the final two hurdles immediately after rewarding his successful run through the tunnel.

Set up a mini-course to begin with. This dog is going from hurdles to long jump.

- Reward at the end.
- Repeat, gradually removing all but the final reward.

PHASE SIX
- Set up another mini-course, e.g. two hurdles, the A-ramp, and another two hurdles.
- Attempt to tackle the course in one go.

- Reward and repeat until confident.
- Slowly introduce hurdles at an angle.
- Gradually add more obstacles.

RUNNING A FULL ROUND
Once you have reached the stage where your dog is able to combine several different obstacles

successfully at the first attempt, you are ready for a complete course. Now you need to practise improving not only your accuracy, but also your speed.

ACCURACY

When you attempt the full round, you should concentrate on maintaining accuracy. If your dog begins to lose accuracy, revert to training the obstacles separately.

SPEED

Timing is very important. With up to 400 competitors in each class, your club is unlikely to present you for competition unless you can complete a clear round in a fast time.

Remember that your dog's speed between the obstacles is likely to be greater than yours. You must take the shortest, quickest course you can, while continuing to guide your dog correctly and confidently around the course.

SPEED TIPS

- Timing begins when your dog crosses the start line, allowing you to cross the line first, without penalty. So, when you begin a round, command your dog to Wait behind the start line while you move forward to the first obstacle, and only then call him on.

- You can also improve your speed by sending your dog ahead of you (the Sendaway), and then redirecting him from a distance. For example, you should Sendaway your dog to the table, while you catch up and count his five seconds on the table. You can then move on to the next obstacle together.

- When redirecting your dog, e.g. "Back", remember to cross *behind* him, so that you do not cause him to slow or to change his step.

- Remember to use reverse turns between obstacles on an angle. This gives you time to get into position ready to guide your dog to the next obstacle. It will prevent your dog from having to take any unnecessary paces to avoid you, thus losing precious seconds.

- Practise jumping each obstacle on corners at an oblique angle. Split-second times can be reduced in this way.

RUNNING A FULL ROUND

Speed is vital, but never at the cost of accuracy. Photos: Sue and Dave Baker.

9 Competition

Having progressed through the various stages of training, you should, by now, be ready for competition.

TYPES OF COMPETITION

There are various types of competition, each open to different categories of entrant. These will vary from country to country, but, as a rough guide, the equivalent to the UK's four class types (listed below) can be found in most countries.

- Progress tests are internal tests which are conducted by your club. They are designed to test the progress which you and your dog have made under instruction.
- Club matches are more competitive, but are restricted to the members of your club. The atmosphere tends to be more relaxed than external competitions, making these events ideal for the novice competitor.

- Limited competitions are open only to those who fulfil certain criteria. Common restrictions on eligibility include geographical area and breed of dog.
- Open competitions, as the name suggests, are open to all, with no restrictions.

JUMPING/AGILITY CLASSES

Within Agility competitions, the tests may consist of Jumping Classes or Agility Classes. Jumping Classes exclude the contact obstacles from the course, whereas Agility classes include them.

RULES AND REGULATIONS

If you belong to an affiliated Agility club, the majority of competitions you attend will be registered with your national kennel club. Accordingly, you must follow the regulations laid

down by your national kennel club. Your Agility club will have a copy of these rules.

KC CLASSES

In the UK, the Kennel Club structures competition using a handicap system. Your dog will be placed in a class according to his Agility-Test success. For details of class structure in other countries, contact your national kennel club.

OTHER CLASSES

The event organisers of Agility competitions will normally structure their classes following the national kennel club's guidelines. However, they are also free to create their own categories. For example, classes may be based on breed (e.g. ABC class – 'Anything But Collies').

Other groups may be based on seniority of age, either that of the dog (veteran class) or that of his handler (golden oldies class). At the other end of the spectrum, there are also classes for juniors (under 12 years old, for example), run by the junior arm of your national kennel club. In the UK, the junior branch of the KC is

Class	Qualification/Handicap
Elementary	For owners, handlers or dogs who have not gained a third prize or above in an Agility and/or a Jumping Class at a licensed Agility Test.
Starters	For owners, handlers or dogs who have not won an Agility/a Jumping Class at a licensed Agility Test (Elementary excepted).
Novice	Open to dogs who are not eligible for Senior and Advanced Classes
Intermediate	Open to all except dogs eligible for Elementary and Starter Classes at a licensed Agility Test.
Seniors	Open to dogs who have won at least two first prizes, one of which must be an Agilty Class at a licensed Agility Test (Elementary and Starter wins excepted).
Advanced	Open to dogs who have won a minimum of four wins at a licensed Agility Test, two of which must be gained in Intermediate, Senior or Open Agility (not Jumping) Classes (Elementary, Starter and Novice wins excepted).
Open	Open to all.

the Kennel Club Junior Organisation (KCJO).

For the novice Agility competitor, there are several 'special' classes, which exclude some of the contact obstacles and are more forgiving with the marks. These classes usually come with names such as the Helter-skelter, Scurry, or Gambler's class.

ENTERING A COMPETITION

Your club and instructor can help you to decide which competitions and classes to enter. Your club will host their own internal competitions and matches, and provide details of other, external shows which you can enter. Alternatively, invitations to enter Agility Tests are advertised in the dog press, including the two specialist Agility magazines, *Agility Voice* and *Agility Eye*.

Once you have made the decision to enter a competition, contact the event organisers to request an entry form and schedule. Read the contents very carefully, before committing yourself – are you and your dog able to cope with the challenge of their particular course? Do not forget to send payment when you return your entry form.

Good preparation for a competition is vital.

BEFORE THE SHOW

Good preparation will help to ensure that your first competition will be a day to remember. Before you leave your home, make sure you have packed your Agility equipment (see page 24), and remember to take plenty of water for your dog and some refreshments for yourself.

A close check is kept on the dog at every obstacle.

ON THE DAY

Make sure you arrive at the competition early. This will give you plenty of time to find a suitable place to park (not having to rush significantly diffuses any stress which you may be feeling).

Book in as soon as you arrive. You will be given a competition schedule and a ring number. Check your schedule carefully. If you are in more than one class, ensure that your timetable does not clash. If it does, speak to one of the stewards. Your ring number should be displayed by pinning it to your clothing. This is important, as failure to display your number correctly is in breach of kennel club rules in most countries.

Use any extra time to find your way around the venue, and to find your class ring. Do not forget to make a note of the nearest exercise area (where your dog may relieve himself), and the human WCs.

Before competition begins, there will be a briefing and course-walking session, which you must attend. Make notes and draw out a plan of your course. Remember that you will be eliminated for taking the wrong route. Ask questions if you are unsure of anything.

THE OFFICIALS

There are inside-the-ring officials and outside-the-ring officials. The inside officials include the judge, who is in overall charge; his scribe, who notes the marks lost; and the jump stewards, who erect knocked-down poles.

The outside officials include the caller, who calls each competitor in turn; the scoreboard steward, who keeps the marks for each competitor, often from the scribe's notes; and the timekeeper, who performs the important function of timing each round.

After you have completed the round, do not forget to thank the officials.

THE ROUND

Take every opportunity to watch others doing their round in your class, paying particular attention to their routes. Observe their interaction with the judge and other officials.

Before you begin your round, make sure you and your dog are fully warmed-up. This reduces the chance of injury, and will help both of you to be more focused.

When your turn comes, one of the stewards will escort you to the ring. Listen to the instruc-tions he gives you, and follow the protocols of the show.

Do your round, and try to remember your training! If you feel a little panicky, do your utmost not to convey this to your dog through your body language. If he detects your nervousness, it may impair his performance, as well as your own.

After the round, check your score and time, and make notes

You can learn from watching other competitors.

Check your score and time after completing your round.

about any areas which you need to improve.

AFTER THE SHOW

Most Agility Tests are run by volunteers, who appreciate a thank you. Help is always needed at these events, and if you are able to contribute, your help at a few shows will be gratefully received. Helping will also give you an invaluable insight into the workings of Agility competitions, which can only help your chances next time.

So, good luck, and now go and compete...

Useful Addresses

THE KENNEL CLUB
1-5 Clarges Street,
Piccadilly,
London W1Y 8AB.
Tel: 0870 606 6750

**THE AMERICAN
KENNEL CLUB**
5580 Centerview Drive,
Raleigh,
NC 27606-3390.
Tel: 212 696 8200.

**NORTH AMERICAN
DOG AGILITY COUNCIL
(NADAC)**
HCR2,
Box 277,
St Maries,
Idaho 83861.

**UNITED STATES DOG
AGILITY ASSOCIATION
(USDAA)**
PO Box 850995,
Richardson,
Texas 75085-0955.

**AGILITY ASSOCIATION
OF CANADA**
RR4,
Lucan,
Ontario NON 2JO.

**AGILITY VOICE
MAGAZINE**
Mr J Gilbert,
100 Bedford Road,
Barton-le-Clay,
Beds MK45 4LR.

AGILITY EYE MAGAZINE
Mr C Park,
3 Ramornie Mill,
Pitlessie,
Fife, KY15 7TH.
Tel: 01337 830649.